OUR
SCHOOLS

STEWART ROSS

Wayland

STARTING HISTORY

Food We Ate
How We Travelled
Our Family
Our Holidays
Our Schools
Shopping
What We Wore
Where We Lived

Picture Acknowledgements
Chapel Studios 6, 8, 9 (top), 12, 15 (top), 17 (top), 21 (top), 23 (top), 27 (top), 28, 29 (top); Eye Ubiquitous 18, 20; S. & R. Greenhill 10; Hulton-Deutsch 7, 9 (bottom), 11, 13, 14, 15 (bottom), 19, 21 (bottom), 24, 25, 27 (bottom), 29, (bottom); Imperial War Museum 16, 17 (bottom); Mary Evans 23 (bottom); Popper 22; Topham 5; Wayland Picture Library 4, 26.

Words that appear in **bold** are explained in the glossary on page 31.

Series Editor: Kathryn Smith
Series Designer: Derek Lee

This edition published in 1994
by Wayland (Publishers) Ltd

First published in 1992 by
Wayland (Publishers) Ltd
61 Western Road, Hove
East Sussex BN3 1JD

© Copyright 1992 Wayland (Publishers) Ltd

British Library Cataloguing in Publication Data
Ross, Stewart
    Our Schools.—(Starting History)
    I. Title   II. Series
    370.941

    HARDBACK ISBN 0-7502-0321-8

    PAPERBACK ISBN 0-7502-1362-0

Typeset by Dorchester Typesetting Group Ltd
Printed and bound in Belgium by Casterman S.A.

Starting History is designed to be used as source material for Key Stage One of the National History Curriculum. The main text and photographs reflect the requirements of AT1 (Understanding history in its setting) and AT3 (Acquiring and evaluating historical information). The personal accounts are intended to introduce different points of view (AT2 – Understanding points of view and interpretations), and suggestions for activities and further research (AT3 – Development of ability to acquire evidence from historical sources) can be found on page 30.

CONTENTS

These children are crossing the road on the way to school. Do you walk to school? Look at the **lollipop man**. What is he doing?

When the lollipop man was your age, schools were very different. This book tells you all about how schools have changed since your parents and grandparents were at school.

These children are walking to school too. Look at the photograph carefully. How can you tell it is not a modern picture? Look at the children's clothes.

The picture was taken in 1936. The lollipop man in the last picture was probably at school then.

OUR SCHOOL

Is your school like this one? It is brand new, with bright classrooms and lots of space for playing.

Not all children go to new schools. Many children go to school in an old building. Do you know how long ago your school was built? See if you can find out.

This classroom was built in 1966. Were your mum and dad at school then?

At that time there were many more children than ever before. Lots of schools were built for them. Some small schools were closed and the pupils moved to bigger ones.

Here is an even older school. It was built before your grandparents were born, but it is still being used.

How can you tell that this is not a new building? Look at the windows and the tower. Do you like old schools or new schools best?

Mary Wheeler went to school in the 1950s. She can remember her classroom very well.

'Our school only had one classroom. It was very tall, with windows like a church. It was dark inside. We all sat in rows of desks, facing Miss Blackmore. The room was heated by the big stove in the picture below. When Miss Blackmore wasn't looking, we used it for drying conkers. In winter it was freezing at the back of the class, so I chose a desk near the stove.'

This school is having a Christmas assembly. It is a **Christian festival**. Do you learn about festivals of other **religions** at school?

Assemblies were different when your grandparents went to school. Ask them what they did in their school assemblies.

Here is a photograph of a school assembly over forty years ago. Do you know anyone who was alive then? The girls are singing a **hymn**.

In those days most assemblies had the same sort of prayers and hymns. In schools today, many children follow different religions. We can learn about different **beliefs** in school assemblies.

COMPUTERS AND CHALK

Do you know what these children are doing? They are working with a **computer**. Do you use computers in your lessons?

Computers are a new **invention**. Your parents did not have them when they were at school. Today we have many special machines at school to help us learn. Can you think of any?

These children are learning to write, using a blackboard and chalk. The picture was taken about forty years ago.

Writing in chalk looks fun, but it was rather messy! What do you use to write?

Does this look like your classroom? Children today do not usually sit at desks in rows, like this. Do you think they look comfortable?

The picture was taken almost sixty years ago. What is the inside of your school classroom like?

Doris Ross is now over seventy years old, but she can still remember her school days.

'There were fifty-five of us at my village school. We did not always have enough books for everyone. When we had a **geography** lesson, we used a big map on the playground wall instead. The teacher took us outside in groups to look at the map. If it rained, we could not have a geography lesson.'

15

What would you do if your school was bombed, like the one in this picture? During the **Second World War** lots of buildings in towns and cities were bombed.

Many children were **evacuated** to the countryside. They left their homes and schools and lived with **foster families**. They went to different schools, until the danger was over.

Ann Morris was a teacher during the war. She remembers wearing a **gas mask** in lessons.

'Don't we look funny! Everyone in school had to carry a gas mask with them all the time. This was in case there was a bomb attack. We had to practise wearing them in lessons, to get used to them. I didn't like mine at all. It smelt horrible and it was difficult to talk when you were wearing it.

These children are working on a **science project**. It is about how their bodies work.

All children study science nowadays. When your parents and grandparents were your age, not everyone learned about science at school. The way we learn, and what we learn about, have changed a lot since then.

These children are making a play in 1966. They are using a tape recorder. Do you use one like this at school?

Thirty years ago, not many primary schools had tape recorders or televisions. Watching television was a special treat. Ask your parents if they had a TV at school.

This boy is reading a book. Does it look like any of the books you use at school?

Books today are very different from the ones used in the past. The books your grandparents read were not very colourful and did not have many pictures. Nowadays books have colour photographs and pictures to make them more interesting and fun.

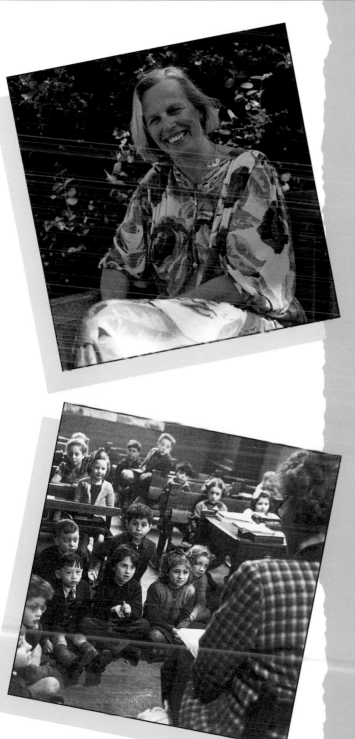

Ann McGregor was at primary school in the 1950s.

'I remember how we learned our times-tables. First we sat on the floor in a group – that's me with a ribbon in my hair. Miss Harper told us which table she wanted. Then we all said together, like a song: "One two is two. Two twos are four . . ." It must have sounded very funny.'

HOLD OUT YOUR HAND!

This teacher looks **stern**, doesn't he? The picture was taken in 1946.

In those days some teachers used to hit naughty pupils with canes, rulers or slippers. This does not happen any more. Are you glad?

Johnny Bell was always in trouble at school. He remembers how he was punished.

'This very old picture reminds me of what happened when I was naughty at school. The teacher read out names of naughty children in class. We had to stand at the front. Then he said: "Bend over". He beat us with his cane. One whack for a little thing wrong. Six for doing something very naughty. It hurt quite a lot, but I suppose it taught me to be good.'

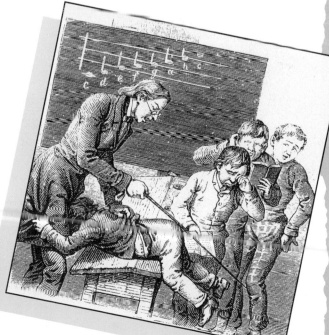

These children are playing in the school playground in 1952. What sort of games do you play at breaktime?

Children's games do not change very much. Your parents probably played hopscotch, football and tag, too. But they did not have computer games!

These boys are doing PE. The photograph was taken about forty-five years ago. How can you tell that it is an old picture? Look at the boys' shorts.

Do you do exercises like this at school? Nowadays most children do sport in PE lessons.

What is happening in this picture? It is school dinner time. Ask a grown-up what they used to eat for dinner at school. Did they like their food?

Today many children take sandwiches, or choose what they want to eat at the canteen, like the children in the picture. Do you know which foods are more healthy to eat?

Peter Downs used to get free milk when he was at school.

'That's me at the back, with short hair. In those days all children were given **one-third** of a pint of milk every morning at break. It was free. I loved my milk. Sometimes other children gave me theirs too. I was very greedy. Children don't get free milk any more, so I'm glad I don't go to school now.'

MOVING ON

This is a large **secondary school** in Sussex. Do you know anyone who goes to secondary school?

100 years ago most children did not go to secondary school. They finished school when they were twelve. Some children started work before that.

Nowadays all children stay at school until they are sixteen.

Chris Fisher thinks schools have changed a lot since he was young.

'I didn't like school. There were more than fifty children in my class. Lessons were very boring. I left school when I was fourteen and got a job. It's really different today. You have TV and **calculators** and computers. The books are better, and I don't think the teachers are so bossy. I'd like to go back to school now. But I think I'm too old. I'm seventy-six!'

Talking to people

You can find out what schools were like by talking to grown-ups. They will tell you all about their school-days. Ask them about buildings, books, lessons, teachers — and punishments!

Making a display

Why not make a scrapbook or display about the history of your school. Try to find out when it was built and what changes have happened. Has it got bigger, or smaller? Has its name changed? Is the uniform the same? Are there any old photographs of the buildings and classes?

Looking at buildings

You can learn a lot about what schools used to be like by looking at old school buildings. Many small schools, built more than 100 years ago, have been turned into homes. Sometimes they still have a small tower for the bell on the top.

Visiting the town library

Ask an adult if they will take you to the local library. There you will be able to find pictures of what the schools in your area used to be like. You may also find some good books.

GLOSSARY

Beliefs   What people believe in, or think is true.

Calculators   Machines which can count.

Christian festival   A celebration, like a party, which is to do with the Christian religion.

Computer   A special machine that helps people with their work.

Evacuated   Moved from a dangerous place to a safe one.

Foster families   Families which look after or bring up a child as their own, for a while.

Gas mask   A special mask to help you breathe when the air is poisoned.

Geography   Learning about the world.

Hymn   A religious song.

Invention   Something made for the first time.

Lollipop man/woman   A person with a round sign who helps children to cross the road safely.

One-third   When something is split up into three parts, each part is called a third.

Religion   Belief in a god or a way to live your life.

Science project   A lot of work on science. Projects are often kept in a folder.

Second World War   The war which lasted from 1939 to 1945. The fighting spread round the whole world.

Secondary school   The school that you go to after primary school.

Stern   Strict or displeased.

INDEX